FAITH:
THE BELIEVERS' ROD

Williams Ekanem

WESTBOW
P R E S S®
A DIVISION OF THOMAS NELSON
& ZONDERVAN

Scripture taken from the Holy Bible, NEW INTERNATIONAL
VERSION®. Copyright © 1973, 1978, 1984 by Biblica, Inc.
All rights reserved worldwide. Used by permission. NEW
INTERNATIONAL VERSION® and NIV® are registered trademarks
of Biblica, Inc. Use of either trademark for the offering of goods or
services requires the prior written consent of Biblica US, Inc.

WestBow Press books may be ordered through booksellers or by contacting:

WestBow Press
A Division of Thomas Nelson & Zondervan
1663 Liberty Drive
Bloomington, IN 47403
www.westbowpress.com
1 (866) 928-1240

ISBN: 978-1-4908-8806-4 (sc)
ISBN: 978-1-4908-8807-1 (e)

Print information available on the last page.

WestBow Press rev. date: 07/23/2015

"God honors faith. Faith is crucial to our walk with God, you need faith to fulfill your destiny."

Pastor E. A. Adeboye
Open Heavens. June 30, 2014

CONTENTS

Chapter 1. Who is a Believer? 1

Chapter 2. The Rod Factor 11

Chapter 3. Understanding Faith 20

Chapter 4. Why do we need a faith lift? 30

Chapter 5. Power of the mind 39

Chapter 6. The Faith Lift 51

Chapter 7. When God Does Not Speak 62

ACKNOWLEDGEMENT

Debbie Macomber, author of "God's Guest List" said that "a book is not the product of the author alone."

This is very true because this book in your hands is a product of a one-day Summer Bible School in 2011 facilitated by me at The Redeemed Christian Church of God, Mercy Seat Chapel in Gaithersburg, Maryland, USA.

In my closing remarks that Saturday afternoon, I promised my audience that God willing, I plan to develop the presentation into a book for a wider audience and for posterity.

I thank God for the realization of the dream. Thank you to all who made the book a reality. In particular, I must mention the brother I met on the road of life's journey, George Oyedele, who stood by me as always to make that seminar successful.

Somehow, I lack adequate words to deeply appreciate Pastor Olaolu Akande, who not only wrote the foreword to this book, but also greatly motivated me with constant assurances that the book, as small as it is, will add value to the reader.

I treasure the patience of my family throughout the period of putting the book together---our children: Judah, Joel and Joseph who didn't really know what daddy was always doing, sitting at the computer, even when they needed attention. The joy is that tomorrow, they will grow to see this as a footprint by dad.

To my wife of inestimable value, I value your understanding, as trying as the times of writing this book was, faith in God of a better tomorrow did it for us.

To God almighty, whose race we are running here on earth, I say thank you Lord for using me as a tool to pass this message of faith to mankind.

FOREWORD

We are people of faith. In good times, in tough times and in changing times, our identity should not change, since the power that drives our faith never changes.

All that God has to offer us, through Christ Jesus is by grace through faith, as Apostle Paul made clear in his epistle to the Ephesians.

Now, Grace is God's own offering to you and faith is our own offering to God. Seen from such a prism, we then can appreciate the crucial factor that faith is, for which reason, Pastor Williams Ekanem has titled this book *Faith: The Believers' Rod.*

It is with your faith that you walk with God, and it is with your faith that you can influence God. It is with your faith that you can impact your world as a believer and it is with your faith that you can draw on the power that is in the name of Jesus!

As the Believers' rod, your faith is not an accessory that beautifies or merely complements. Even though it ultimately does those things, but it has far too much more to offer! Our faith is our balance, our stay, and by it we hold sway!

The treatment that the Pastor and Journalist Ekanem has given this central subject of our relationship with the LORD is comprehensive and insightful.

I personally find Pastor Ekanem a gifted teacher of the word with very notable revelations from the throne of grace.

This book is a reflection of his depth and the richness of his insight into the word of God by the gifting of the Holy Spirit.

In seven concise chapters, the author has managed to put together a book that can richly bless your walk of faith, inspire you afresh and recharge the power of God in you. It is very reader-friendly and you can retune your reading habit by relishing the power-packed teachings in this book.

It is not possible to read this book and not become generally more enlightened as a Believer.

It would in fact give you a faith lift as the title of one of the chapters promised. It can spur your Christian life and clarify many issues that bother many a Believer today.

Wherever you may be today as a person of faith, this book will refresh you. In good times, this book will further build your faith; in tough times the book will restore hope, and in changing times, the book points to an unchangeable changer-the one who is the same yesterday, today and forever!

Jesus is LORD!

Laolu Akande
Executive Director
Christian Association of
Nigerian-Americans, CANAN
Bayshore, New York
USA

CHAPTER 1

WHO IS A BELIEVER?

As a teacher of the word in my local church, I have attempted to answer this very question so many times. Almost always, the vague expressions on faces of the people show they would have wanted more explanation and clarification.

For some inexplicable reasons, a direct answer that a Believer is anyone who believes in the death and resurrection of Jesus Christ always seems very simplistic to some, yet it is the truth.

Considering the tedious process and sacrifice it takes to be initiated into a cult, secret societies and the like, most new comers to the Kingdom of God often wonder how simple it is to become a Believer, by just renouncing our sins, confessing them and receiving a new life under the banner of Jesus Christ.

Notwithstanding the number of times one has and will continue to touch on this subject, one thing is certain and that is, a Believer or Christian is a follower of Jesus Christ.

As a follower of Christ, the individual should also be a disciple. It follows naturally that a follower is first and foremost a Believer.

A Believer is one who professes Jesus Christ as Lord and Savior. The scriptures state this explicitly in Romans 10:9-11, *"That if you <u>confess with your mouth</u>, Jesus is Lord, and <u>believe in your heart</u> that God <u>raised him from the dead</u>, you <u>will be saved</u>. For it is with your heart that you believe and are justified, and it is with your mouth that you confess and are saved."* (NIV)

The above verse quickly brings to mind the confessions made at baptism. Usually before the immersion at baptism, the conducting minister would normally ask what the individual believes. The individual to be baptized will say, I believe that Jesus Christ is the son of God, my Lord and Savior," following that, another question will be, what is your confession? The respondent will answer that he or she 'confesses that Jesus Christ died on the cross for the remission of our sins.'

Without taking the well beaten path in discussing who a Believer is or should be, let us take a closer look at the above Bible text, pick out the underlined phrases and consider them one after the other.

Confess with your mouth: Confession of sins for forgiveness and confession of faith in God are outstanding characteristics in the life of a Believer. The entire Bible is replete with the need for sincere confession of sins and guilt. David showed a clear example in Psalm 32: 5 where he insisted in confessing his sins to the Lord for forgiveness. A true confession brings mercy from God and gives the individual a fresh start in the walk with God.

A sincere confession is however that which is accompanied by a complete turn around from the sinful act, else it would be as a dog going back to its vomit and it would have been better if the individual did not know the way of righteousness in the first instance. 2 Peter 2: 21-22.

It is a very dangerous thing to accept salvation and then go back to one's sinful nature. The most culprits here are usually those who practice self righteousness and not the righteousness of God at the first instance.

The very interesting thing about confession is that God looks at the heart and can therefore know an insincere confession. In his first epistle, Apostle John clarified any iota of doubt about our sinful nature by stating that "if *we claim to be without sin, we deceive ourselves and the truth is not in us. But on the other hand, if we confess our sins, He is faithful and just to and will forgive us our sins and purify us from all unrighteousness.*" John 8:9

Besides confessing our sins, we also confess our faith. To confess one's faith is to acknowledge the truth about Jesus Christ. Faith in God is not like an earthly treasure that one must guide jealously to avoid infringement, theft or trespassing. A true Believer lives a life of faith and is duty bound to confess Christ at any point in time. This way, the Believer will be carrying out the great commission given to

Believers in Mathew 28:19 to *"therefore go and make disciples of all nations."*

It therefore means that any Believer that does not practically confess Jesus Christ with his/her mouth is still lacking in the spiritual responsibility because the Bible says *"whoever acknowledges me before others, I will also acknowledge before my father in heaven."* Mathew 10:32

A good example of the Believers confession is as shown in the meeting with His disciples when Simon Peter answered and said, *"You are the Messiah, the Son of the living God."*

"Jesus replied, blessed are you, Simon son of Jonah, for this was not revealed to you by flesh and blood, but by my Father in heaven. And I tell you that you are Peter, and on this rock I will build my church, and the gates of Hades will not overcome it." Mathew 16:16-18

Believe in your heart: Human life is centered in the heart, Proverbs 4:23 describes the heart as the wellspring of life. God looks at the heart of the Believer to know its motive and true devotion. It therefore goes without saying that anyone who pays lip service to the things of God or indulges in eye service for the approval of men, Galatians 1:10 cannot be said to be a true Believer of Christ.

At the healing of the paralytic, the Pharisees and the teachers started thinking about how to implicate Jesus Christ, but He quickly told them as shown in Luke 5: 22, *"why are you thinking these things in your hearts?"*

A lot of things go on in our minds, both positive and negative based on our experiences, world view, environment, companion etc. The heart controls human emotions, will and intelligence, therefore God takes a good look at the heart at every point in time to know the genuineness of every act, or lack of it.

The Bible says that *"the heart is deceitful above all things and beyond cure,"* Jeremiah 17:9, but through regeneration, the Believers' heart is softened, recreated and purified by God to produce good fruit and a life of obedience to the will and commands of God.

Conscious of the deceitfulness of the heart, David said in Psalm 139: 23-24 that God should search his heart so that he can be on the right path.

With a corrupted heart, a positive confession is hard to make, because it is out of the abundance of the heart that the mouth speaks.

The New Testament tells us that those who accept Jesus Christ become new people in the eyes of God. All who admit their sins and confess them, believe in Christ as their sin bearer are given a whole new heart, way of thinking and they become children of God.

To have a right heart towards God, Pastor Enoch Adeboye the General Overseer of The Redeemed Christian Church of God in Open Heavens volume 11 said one must allow God to try your heart, test your motives and motivations because as he puts it, "it is after your heart is tried and

5

directed by the Holy Spirit that your desires can blend with God's will and purpose."

Raised from the Dead: Here lies the line between the Christian faith and all others. A genuine Believer holds on to the death and resurrection of Jesus Christ with an unequivocal conviction.

The resurrection of Jesus Christ is the basis of the Believers' faith, because without it, Christians would be lost and our faith would be useless and misplaced.

Apostle Paul told the people in Corinth that, *"if Christ has not been raised, our preaching is useless and so is your faith."* 1 Corinthians 15: 14

The entire New Testament affirms that Jesus Christ was crucified, buried and resurrected on the third day. From the Christians standpoint, this happened to fulfill the scriptures. Christ's resurrection declares His deity, assures us of an acceptance by Him, and proves His victory over death and the powers of darkness. Resurrection gives Believers a living hope, and guarantees our eventual resurrection at His second coming.

Scriptures promise that someday Christians will also rise from the dead and receive a new body like Christ's.

There are actually two points to be noted in resurrection, first is the resurrection of Jesus Christ and second is the resurrection when Christ returns, that is at the second coming.

This is why Jesus Christ said in John 14: 1-2 *"Do not let your hearts be troubled. You believe in God; believe also in me. My Father's house has many rooms; if that were not so, would I have told you that I am going there to prepare a place for you?"*

Jesus is too faithful to say that He would come again and then doesn't. He will surely come again, not by our own timing but on an unknown day and time set by His father. Not everyone would be alive to witness that day and that is why it is often said that the day anyone dies is akin to the day Jesus returns to that person because there is no repentance or confession in the grave.

It is surprising that people still either ignore or find it difficult to believe this truth. Those still finding it difficult to believe should look at it this way; the prophets of old prophesized that Jesus will come, He came, Jesus Himself prophesized His death and resurrection and it came to pass. Now if all these have taken place, then the truth that He will come again should be without a doubt to any discerning individual.

You will be Saved: To seek and receive salvation through the grace of God is the ultimate goal of any Believer. To Believers, no one can be saved from sin, except he or she receives Jesus Christ as a personal savior.

The scripture says that *"salvation is found in no one else, for there is no other name under heaven given to mankind by which we must be saved."* Acts 4: 12

The import of the above verse is that without accepting Jesus Christ as one's personal Savior, the person is hell bound. The process of salvation starts with admitting your sinful nature, confession of sins, forsaking them and inviting the Lord Jesus into one's heart.

To admit and confess one's sins is the very first step to salvation as *"All have sinned and fall short of the glory of God,"* Romans 3: 23. Nobody is saved by trying to be good, we are saved by grace. *"For it is by grace you have been saved, through faith-and this is not from yourselves, it is the gift of God."* Ephesians 2:8

As simple as this may sound, that is the way it is, and that is why in Christendom, it is said that the most important thing, (salvation) is free. There is no sacrifice, no initiation of any sort, no payment of fees, it has to do with taking a personal decision and making it fast before it is too late, since no one knows tomorrow.

A yearning and repentant person does not need any specially prepared statement; the words to say are surely not a citation or repetition of any creed, they are not an incantation.

The tax collector in Luke 18: 13 for instance did not have to recite any creed, all he said was *"God, have mercy on me a sinner."* The difference is that he said it with all his body, soul and spirit. The Bible records that he did not even lift his eyes to heaven, not looking around to see who is there or not there, but beat his heart to show brokenness.

Many people, especially youths have toyed with their salvation, because of what the next person, family, colleagues, contemporaries, boss, subordinates etc would say.

The story of Nicodemus quickly comes to mind here. In John 3:2, Nicodemus went to Jesus by night, apparently ashamed or afraid of what those who know him would say if seen with Jesus in daylight.

The shame of being identified with Christ has robbed people of the gift of salvation and as a Preacher once said, those who respond to the call to salvation in a secluded place or when people are asked to close their eyes, so as not to be seen making public confession, constitute the lazy Christians today. The reasoning here is that from the onset the boldness to receive and confess Christ was lacking. They are shy of identifying with Christ in the public.

To such people, the Bible warns that *"If anyone is ashamed of me and my words in this adulterous and sinful generation, the Son of Man will be ashamed of them when he comes in his Father's glory with the holy angels."* Mark 8: 38

Note that the tax collectors' confession was very different from that of one of the criminals who was hung with Jesus. While the other criminal was busy mocking Jesus as most people do today (when we commit sins), the other, made a simple confession, *"Jesus, remember me when you come into your kingdom,"* to which Jesus replied instantly, *"truly I tell you, today you will be with me in paradise."* Luke 23: 39-43

Depending on the individual and the congregation, a typical confession may be "Lord Jesus I have sinned against you, have mercy on me and accept me into your kingdom. For I believe that Jesus is the son of God, who came and died for me and rose from the dead for my sake. I now accept Jesus as my Lord and personal savior."

Action Point

Do that now, if you have not had the opportunity to do so before and be welcomed into the kingdom of light, for you are now a new creature.

This decision and action becomes very necessary at this stage of this book, for it is only then, that the discussion in subsequent chapters will make meaning to you.

CHAPTER 2

THE ROD FACTOR

The Hebrew word for "rod" is "Matteh." "Matteh" which means a branch. Throughout the scriptures, the Bible places a high premium on the use of a rod, either as scepter, which shall not depart from the hand of Judah in Genesis 49:10; or the rod of correction in Proverbs.

The rod could also be a staff, a kind of support as the Psalmist pointed out that God's rod and staff comforts him in Psalm 23.

In Exodus 4:17, God told Moses the significance of the rod in his hand and what it would be used to accomplish, *"take this staff in your hand so you can perform the signs with it."*

True to those words, it was when Moses held up the rod that Israel prevailed over the Amalekites, and when his hand became weary and he lowered it that the Amalekites prevailed. God used the rod in Moses' hand to declare the plagues upon Egypt. The rod was what Moses used in parting the red sea for the Israelites to cross over to the other side. It was also the rod that struck the rock and brought out water for the Israelites.

Although many people used the rod in the Bible, like the rod of Aaron, rod of Levi but the rod of Moses turns out the most referred, apparently due to the history behind that vey rod.

The Internet Sacred Text Archive (ISTA), a website dedicated to the preservation of electronic public domain texts, including the Bible states that when Adam and Eve were driven out of the garden, "Adam, as if knowing that he was never to return to his place, cut off a branch from the tree of good and evil--which is the fig-tree--and took it with him and went forth; and it served him as a staff all the days of his life."

The archive recollected that after the death of Adam, his son Seth took it, for there were no weapons as yet at that time. This rod, according to the recount, was passed on from hand to hand unto Noah and from Noah to Shem; and it was then handed down from Shem to Abraham as a blessed thing from the Paradise of God.

With this rod, it is was recorded that Abraham broke the images and graven idols which his father made, and that accounted for why God said to him, 'Get thee out of thy father's house."

Abraham clutched this rod every where he went, as far as Egypt, and from Egypt to Palestine. With the death of Abraham, Isaac took it, and (it was handed down) from

Isaac to Jacob; and with the rod, Jacob fed the flocks of Laban the Aramean in Paddan Aram.

The record from ISTA adds that after Jacob, Judah his fourth son took over the rod. It is the same rod that Judah gave to Tamar his daughter-in-law, with his signet ring and his napkin, as the pay for what he had done. From him (it came) to Pharez.

According to the record, at this time, "there were wars everywhere, and an angel took the rod, and laid it in the Cave of Treasures in the mount of Moab, until Midian was built."

From when the angel took it, it was away until another generation. Then there was in Midian a man, upright and righteous before God, according to the story whose name was Yathrô (Jethro).

Jethro is said to have come in contact with the rod in a cave when he was feeding his flock on the mountain.

He is said to have found the cave and took the rod by divine agency; and he kept it until his old age. It therefore happened that when he gave his daughter to Moses, he said to him, 'Go in, my son, take the rod, and go forth to thy flock.' When Moses had set his foot upon the threshold of the door, the account added that " an angel moved the rod, and it came out of its own free will towards Moses. And Moses took the rod, and it was with him until God spoke with him on mount Sinai."

In the process of time, it was the same rod that Moses used when God said to him, Cast the rod upon the ground, he did so, and it became a great serpent; and the Lord said, 'Take it,' and he did so, and it became a rod as at first."

Although with a slight variation, but same storyline of the transfer of the rod from Adam to Moses, there is another account from Pirke D'Rebbe Eliezer 40 (a Midrashic work composed by the school of Rebbe Eliezer ben Hyrcanus) in "The Staff of Moses" by Hillel ben David.

He gave the origin of this amazing staff in this way, "Created at twilight, before the Sabbath, it was given to Adam in the Garden of Eden. Adam gave it to Chanoch (Enoch), who gave it to Metushelach (Methuselah); he in turn passed it on to Noach (Noah). Noach bequeathed it to his son Shem, who transmitted it to Avraham (Abraham)."

According to this account from David, the rod moved from Avraham to Yitzchak (Isaac), and then to Yaaqov (Jacob), who took it with him to Egypt. Ya'aqov gave it to Yosef (Joseph); and upon Yosef's death, all his possessions were removed to Pharaoh's place. Yitro (Jethro) one of Pharaoh's advisors desired it, whereupon he took it and stuck it in the ground in his garden in Midian. From then on no one could pull out the staff until Moshe came.

This account indicated that Moses read the Hebrew letters on the staff, and pulled it out readily. Knowing then that Moshe (Moses) was the redeemer of Israel, Yitro gave him his daughter Tziporra (Zepporah) in marriage." Then, as a shepherd to Yitro, it was while investigating the phenomenon of the Burning Bush, that <u>HaShem</u> said to Moshe: Shemot What is in your hand? And he (Moshe) said, 'a staff'."

Moses' deep rooted doubts as expressed in Exodus 3 is said to have led to the introduction of the rod by God with the question, "*what is that in your hand,*" Exodus 4:2 for which Moses answered *"a rod."*

Just as it happened to Moses, we do most times underrate what we have. Moses while tending his in-law's sheep had a rod, which to him, was like any ordinary piece of wood, but God demonstrated here as ever, that He can use what we have for His glory.

More often than not, we always consider what we have as insignificant, but when God breathes on it, one with God becomes majority. God did same with Shamgar in Judges 3: 31, with Samson in Judges 15:15, with David in 1 Samuel 17:49, with the widow in 2 Kings 4:2 and also with the young lad in John 6:9-10 amongst others.

There Shall Come Forth a Rod

More succinctly, prophet Isaiah in 11.1 referred to the rod as a branch from the root of Jesse, which refers to Jesus Christ. The prophet creates here, an image of a small tender branch that could be easily broken, yet shall conquer death, be victorious, redeem His people and become in modern times the author and finisher of our faith.

Bible scholars say the rod of Moses was a type of Christ. This is because at the appointed time, one whom the rod represented appeared.

Writing on "The Rod of Moses" Jerry Healan stated that "The Rod of Moses is an instrument of the Scriptures that has not been focused on. The neglect has caused us to suffer a tremendous lack of knowledge concerning Biblical truths."

According to Healan, a study into the significance of the rod, will reveal to us a greater understanding and reaffirm the faith of many, as to who the Messiah really is.

Whether or not the history of the rod recounted earlier holds any water, the fact remains that in whatever form of worship or religion, people do always need something to hold on to.

In traditional religions across the globe, followers always need a handle, something to carry, wear or fall back on. In want of what to hold on to for a psychological satisfaction, some have kept amulets in their homes, offices, cars and even wear them.

More often than not, people rate the efficacy of their chosen religion on the power of whatever they hold on to. The African traditional religions offer good examples where a variety of objects, talisman are in use.

This may have been why for instance, the Israelites in Exodus 32 gave out their earrings, trinkets, and other jewels to Aaron who created the molded calf they wanted to depend on.

Even some Christians today cling more to their cross, beads, rosary, candles, handkerchief more than the name of Jesus, which is more than any other name. Such people end up idolizing the creation than worshiping the creator, Romans 1:25.

With this tendency to have something to hold on to, feel and touch, fall back on, the question then arise, what does the Believer, the true disciple of Christ hold on to?

First and foremost, it must be noted that *"God is spirit, and his worshippers must worship in spirit and in truth"* John 4:24. True Believers do NOT need any visible physical object to hold on to except looking unto Jesus as the perfecta of our faith and making Him the originator of our faith.

Mathew Henry's Commentary puts it this way: "He is the finisher of grace and of the work of faith with power in the souls of His people; and He is the judge and the rewarder of our faith."

Faith, in the redeeming power of Jesus is the best substance any Believer needs to hold on to.

Just as Moses' rod which God used to perform wonders, faith stands out as that substance, handle, object and confidence that the Believer has. Often referred to as the currency of heaven, faith can move mountains; it serves as the abiding link between the Believer and his savior.

Daniel in the Lion's den did not have any object, talisman, waved or flashed anything to demobilize the Lion, nor did

David burn any candle, spit or dangle anything to daze Goliath.

In both instances, they had absolute faith in the saving power of God, the type of faith the men who opened up a roof to let down the paralytic had in the healing power of Jesus. Also the Centurion who was confident with Jesus just saying the word without going to his house to heal the servant.

Here lies the difference between the Believer and the unbeliever. A Believer believes before he/she sees, while the unbeliever wants to feel, touch before believing. The scriptures make this even clearer when Jesus told Thomas, one of the twelve disciples that, *"blessed are those who have not seen and yet have believed."* John 20:29

As an invisible but inevitable substance for God's own people, faith can therefore be said to be the Believers' Rod. It is what the Believer holds on to irrespective of circumstance, so as to please God. Just as Abraham believed God and earned the prefix of the father faith.

Don't get stuck with hopelessness or negative attitude like the man in John 5:7, but rather make yourself a prisoner of hope as advised by Zachariah 9:12; as it paid off for the disciples of old, it will pay off for you in Jesus mighty name.

Apostle Paul in his letter to the Romans said that faith triumphs in trouble and pointed out that

"Therefore, since we have been justified through faith, we have peace with God through our Lord Jesus Christ, [2] through whom we have gained access by faith into this grace in which we now stand. And we boast in the hope of the glory of God." Romans 5:1-2.

But what really is faith?

CHAPTER 3

UNDERSTANDING FAITH

A complete trust, confidence, unquestioning, especially on religious belief or creed is how the American Century dictionary defines faith.

Going forward however, we would consider faith in relation to the experiential knowledge of the individual.

As Believers in the death and resurrection of our Lord Jesus Christ, the meaning and reason of putting one's faith in God could be as varied as the individuals giving the definition.

To some people, faith is absolute trust in God; a complete, total, no-holds back attitude. This is very different from just a trust in dad, mum, uncle, in-law, boss, friend or god-father. People in this category have an unconditional faith in God and do not consider it misplaced because to them, unlike man, God is faithful to do what He says and says what He does. These people hold tenaciously to the scriptures as in Isaiah 55: 10-11, where the Bible assures that God's word will not return empty but must accomplish His desire.

Some people may not be spirit filled, tongue speaking, demon casting Christians, but they have a resolute faith in God. Maybe because they do not have well-endowed and connected individuals to look up to, or somehow, may have gotten their fingers burnt in relying on people.

Another group of Believers exercise this supreme faith in God when they remember that there is indeed a curse on anybody who trusts in man as pointed out by Prophet Jeremiah in his seventeenth chapter, verse five and indeed another biblical revelation that states that without faith, it is impossible to please God.

Practically, if you can decipher why you should put your faith in God Almighty, you can then determine to hold very tenaciously to it.

Some consider faith as waiting on God to Act: The examples in 1 King 18:1-40 where Elijah taunted the prophets of Baal and Daniel 3 concerning the three Hebrew young men are topical examples of the faith that waits on God to act. *"If we are thrown into the blazing furnace, the God we serve is able to save us from it, and He will rescue us from your hand O king."* Daniel 3:17. Those were the words of the three Hebrew boys.

They displayed outright confidence in the ability of God to save them, but even if He doesn't, they will still glorify Him, they disclosed to the apparent shock of many then and even now.

Ordinarily, if some worldly wise fellows had been told to bow to lesser gods, verbally they would say no way, but before long, they bend, pretending to be adjusting their shoe lace whereas in reality, they were stylishly bowing to Nebuchadnezzar's gods.

Most often, we pretend to be serving or worshiping God, paying lip service or eye service, while in reality, we are worshiping man for fear of the repercussion of doing otherwise.

Faith is resting in the Lord: As important as physical rest is, spiritual rest is even more important and beneficial. Hebrews 4:3 tells us that believers enter His rest by surrendering everything unto Him. Jesus Christ said *"come to me all you who are weary and burdened and I will give you rest."* Mathew 11:28. There is a spiritual and emotional rest, sense of peace and serenity which is experienced when one turns to God for everything.

In overcoming your Goliath, just as David did, you need to learn to rest in His might, not your credentials or network because the arms of flesh do fail. Remember, it is not by your power or might but by His spirit.

People that exercise their faith through resting in Him and handing it all over to God are candidates for miracles, irrespective of circumstances. Robert Schuler says it this way, "our faith leads us to victory every time we rest in God's hands," and Tommy Brant counsels that "faith is simply when you bring God into the picture."

All great achievers in the Bible were ordinary people like us, but they all had one thing in common, they stepped out in faith and rested in the ability of God to see them through.

Ramona Carol, as cited by John Mason's book <u>The Impossible is Possible</u> defines faith as **Putting all your eggs in God's basket** and counting your eggs before they are hatched. Abraham put his most prized possession-Isaac on the line in Genesis 22:1-2. For three days, he and his only son travelled for the sacrifice. Isaac, in this circumstance, represented all his eggs through which the promised generation would come, but was here, being led to the slaughter. In the nick of time, God intervened; He usually will intervene when we make a commitment, not before. That is why we are today still reading about Ruth in the Bible, a woman whose exceptional sense of commitment to her mother in-law placed her on the lineage of Jesus Christ.

It is also apt to add that commitment comes with risk, there is always the risk factor to deal with in making a commitment, which explains why Esther for instance said, *"if I perish, I perish" Esther 4:16*

In 1 Kings 17:7-24, the widow at Zarephath put all the food and drink she had in one basket giving them to the man of God, and it paid off for her.

Faith is like a Toothbrush: However strong the love is between couples, when they travel, they pick their individual toothbrushes; so with the children. This is because, surely, nobody prefers using another person's toothbrush, except maybe one forgets his or her own and cannot readily get another one.

This is what faith should be, everyone should have a level of faith and use it daily; *"whoever wants to be my disciple must deny themselves and take up their cross daily and follow me"* Luke 9:23. The scripture here advises us to carry our cross daily.

The cross is not by any means a bed of roses, it is still rugged, denoting trials and temptations. One of the great faith teachers, George Miller (1805-1898) pointed out that "trials are the food of faith," and counseled Believers to persevere during tough times.

The implication here is that just as we use our toothbrush daily, we must also muster faith to deal with our daily trials because as Schuler puts it, " your finest hour will grow out of your greatest burden, with God all things are possible."

Faith is also how big or small your God is: How mighty or otherwise your perception of God is explains some peoples' definition of faith. Is He the omnipotent, omnipresent and omniscience God we read about?

Is He only God of the good times, and not of the tough times. According to Fred Kinsey in <u>What to Do When Your World Falls Apart</u>, "the way you answer the above questions may have a lot to do with how strong or weak your faith is."

In Daniel 3:18, the Hebrew boys did not demand that God proves Himself to them, they were willing to accept God's will, whatever it meant for them. Wow!

They had a faith that was willing to accept whatever came their way as being part of God's plan for their lives and their faith. And they were richly rewarded.

Prophet Elijah in 1 Kings 17 wouldn't have bothered carrying the dead son of the widow into the upper room, if he wasn't sure that the God he believes in would not raise him from dead.

The officials would have succeeded in quieting the blind man in Luke 18 if he had a small perception of Jesus Christ, but he defied them and shouted the more, *"Jesus, son of David, have mercy on me"* Luke 18: 38 and he did receive his sight. Your faith will work for you in Jesus name.

If you are serving God and you deeply believe God can make the seemingly impossible possible in your situation, then you can put anything on the line knowing that it cannot fail.

Faith is the substance of things hoped for, the evidence of things not seen: As familiar as this definition of faith from Hebrews 11:1 could be, there are two aspects as elucidated in Mathew Henry's Bible Commentary, that is still worth considering.

One, as a substance of things hoped for, faith is a firm persuasion and expectation that God will perform all that

He has promised us in Christ. It may take longer than we anticipate, but Romans 4: 21 encourages us to be fully convinced that what He had promised, He is also able to perform.

Secondly, as evidence of things not seen, faith demonstrates to the mind's eye, the reality of those things that cannot be discerned by the human eyes. That is why Jesus told Thomas, *"Blessed are those who have not seen and yet have believed."* John 20:29

Faith as a substance of things not seen, sees the invisible, believes the incredible and receives the impossible.

This becomes even more cogent when we get to realize that sight is synonymous with doubt. This is why people inspect goods several times before they pay for it. That cognitive dissonance comes into play and they doubt the choice they are making at that particular time, although they see and hold the item.

In most cases, even after buying the item, some people would still need a second opinion to either confirm or erase their doubts about the item that they already own.

What Faith is not

Faith is NOT Presumption: Presumption is a guess; something you think is true because it is very likely to be true.

A typical case of acting on presumption rather than on faith is exemplified here, *"Nevertheless, in their presumption they went up toward the highest point in the hill country, though neither Moses nor the ark of the LORD's covenant moved from the camp. Then the Amalekites and the Canaanites who lived in that hill country came down and attacked them and beat them down all the way to Hormah."* Numbers 14:44-45

As is usual with acting on presumption, the Israelites were woefully defeated when they went to war on the presumption that they would win, because they had been winning.

David Stoop in You Are What You Think puts it very aptly that "presumption rushes out ahead of God, demand results, while faith simply rests, leaving the outcome in God's hand."

God has the prerogative to heal, give, and deliver, not you. It is presumption to think that God is duty bound to reach out to you. In Romans 9: 15 God told Moses, *"I will have mercy on whom I will have mercy."*

Daniel 4: 25 says explicitly that He is a sovereign God and gives to anyone He chooses.

Exercising faith does not in any way mean dictating to God. Just as God Almighty is not a magician, Stoop argues that "God cannot be put into any genie box and cannot be predicted on any particular formula."

Presumption demands, while faith rests. God does not owe anyone, when we make demands, placing God at our beck and call; the most we can get is self-imposed frustrations.

Presumption is being forward, trying to help God. 2 Samuel 6:6-7. Faith as exemplified in Lamentations 3: 25-26, 31-33, simply rests, leaves the result in God's able hands.

Faith is NOT an Impression: An impression is a feeling, an idea or intuition. This is very far from faith.

Paul King in his book, <u>Moving Mountains</u> stated that, "to those with an illness or injury, do not rise from your bed or walk on your lame foot because somebody tells you to do so. That isn't faith but impression."

At the very best, that can be a blind faith because it is without the unction or leading of the Holy Spirit.

Even when God spoke to Gideon, to be sure, he still requested for a sign, Judges 6: 17, 39. We must be able to distinguish from what we need and the plan of God, because what you think you really need may after all not be God's plan for you.

God will only honor His word or plan and not your wishful thinking. Abraham, the father of faith heard from God before departing from Haran. God told David to pursue that he would overtake; just as the Centurion's servant was healed because of absolute believe in the spoken word of God.

We need to receive a clear word and inspiration from God in taking steps of faith.

Faith is NOT an Impulse: Impulse is a desire, fancy, an imagination.

Impulse is fleeting; it will soon fade whereas faith in God endures as the word becomes living. Even when the promise is forgotten by man, the Holy Spirit brings it to remembrance and prompts action.

Over two years since the chief butler forgot Joseph in the prison, the Holy Spirit prompted him to remember Joseph when nobody could interpret Pharaoh's dreams in Genesis 41.

Those who mistakenly consider faith as an impulse are often terribly disappointed when their faith is being tested. Such people do not know that trials are actually the food of faith; one can only be found faithful after passing the faith test as in the case of Abraham.

For a three day journey, so many people would have discontinued the journey as reflected in Genesis 22 when the object of sacrifice was his son, his only son, Hebrews 11:17, but he continued the faith walk until God intervened. The Lord will intervene for you in Jesus name.

You will experience divine intervention as you genuinely put your faith in Him.

CHAPTER 4

WHY DO WE NEED
A FAITH LIFT?

Paul King (2004) points out that faith will not remove all the puzzles and uncertainties of life, but that faith makes us realize that answers are found in God's sovereign purposes.

For instance, Job never received answers from God to all his questions about his suffering, yet he came to understand that God is greater.

"Maturity is to understand that you don't have to understand, "King pointed out. We must admit even when in the midst of our wilderness experience that, when one is down to nothing, then God is up to something.

Satan, the hinderer may build a barrier around us, but he can never roof us in such that we cannot look up to the author and finisher of our faith Jesus Christ, unless we cooperate with Satan by giving up, losing our faith in the saving power of God.

We therefore need a faith lift because **faith is the Channel through which Grace of God flows**: A channel is a medium that facilitates something to move from point A to B. it could be current, message, correspondence, goods, services etc.

Since the grace of God (receiving what one does not deserve) is key in the Christian race, therefore it is faith that takes mercy, blessings, healing, the word etc to the believer, when we ask in prayer.

The faith of the Syro-Phonecian woman in Mark 7: 24-30 became the channel through which her child received deliverance from demonic attack.

Jesus even commended the "great faith" of the Centurion who in Luke 7:7 told Jesus not to come to his house, but just say the word.

Faith Energizes Prayer: in all intents and purpose, faith and prayer go hand in hand. Prayer is nothing more than an expression of faith in our Lord and savior.

We get more on this relationship between faith and prayer when Jesus explained that, *"therefore I tell you, whatever you ask for in prayer, believe that you have received it, and it will be yours."* Mark 11:24

Jesus opened that communication situation earlier in verse 22 of Mark 11 by saying, *"have faith in God."* James, a disciple best known for his fervent prayers, in his writings,

James 5: 15 establishes the truth that prayers offered in faith produces results.

As E.M Bonds puts it, true prayer then is an operation of faith, "genuine prayer is praying with faith. There is said to be no real prayer without faith and no faith without prayer."

Faith is not only expressed through prayer, but prayer actually energizes and activates faith. According to John Mason, "prayer is asking for rain, faith is carrying the umbrella."

This is akin to testimonies of women who with absolute faith go for maternity shopping; buying baby clothes and accessories with the very strong faith that God will bless them with fruit of the womb.

This writer has seen instances of such demonstration of faith and it paid off for the women. Your absolute faith in the Lord Jesus Christ will pay off for you too.

Faith gives courage to face the present with confidence and future with expectancy:

To Abraham, his faith hinged on the faithfulness of God. That is why the scriptures say in Romans 4:20 that Abraham did not waiver at the promise but continued to give glory to God, even after 25 years.

Paul added quickly in the next verse, Romans 4:21 that, *"being fully persuaded that God had power to do what he had promised,"* is a sure indication that His promises in our lives will come to pass. It does not matter how long it takes, as nobody, no power can thwart the will of God almighty. This is more so, when Colossians 2: 10 reveals that God is the head of all principalities and powers.

It must be pointed out that in all cases; it is not always the promises of God that fails, but our faith that fails when we waiver.

Mathew Henry's Bible Commentary explains further that, "Abraham just like some of us, saw the storms of doubts, fears, temptations likely to rise against the promise. But Abraham, having taken God for his pilot, and the promise for his card and compass, like a bold adventurer sets up all sails, regards neither winds or clouds but trust to the wisdom and faithfulness of his pilot and bravely makes it to the harbor."

According to John Mason, it is usually not so much the greatness of our troubles as the smallness of our faith that causes us to complain and grumble.

Hebrews 4:2 emphasizes that **faith gives value to scriptures**. *" For we also have had the good news proclaimed to us, just as they did; but the message they heard was of no value to them, because those who heard did not combine it with faith."*

Apostle Paul wondered how people can believe in Him of whom they have not heard, stressing that faith comes by hearing the word of God. Romans 10:17

We should constantly feed our faith by reading, hearing and meditating on the word of God. However, the question here is how do we use the word we have? The question is for those who read the word anyway.

As it is, one can only make use of that which is useful, profits and adds value. But come to think of it, we deliberately expose ourselves to the news media and make effective use of the news, weather reports, traffic reports because they are considered to be of value.

Do the scriptures add such value to our life? Do we make deliberate effort to read the word of God daily? Are the scriptures in any way useful to our daily living? James 1:22-24 encourages us not to merely listen, but act on the word of God so that it can add value to our life.

We must expose ourselves to the word through hearing or reading, believe it and let it increase our faith. This will help us to effectively appropriate the knowledge and power of Christ in us.

Some of us are very zealous for God, but our zeal needs to be backed by knowledge as Romans 10:2 instructs that, *"for I can testify about them that they are zealous for God, but their zeal is not based on knowledge."*

As a Preacher once said, "the knowledge, faith that you have not acquired in the daytime, you cannot use in the night," and I add here—(especially in the day or time of trouble). Remember that the day of trouble is inevitable; remember Job warned us that man is of a few days and full of trouble.

Whatever is not from faith is sin. Apostle Paul did not mince words in Romans 14:23 when he made this revelation. Since the other side of faith is doubt and fear, whatever is not done in faith is sin. Mason explains that fear is faith that it won't work out.

Doubt is real; it sees the obstacle, so also is fear. Doubt and fear could be valid and justified, they afflicted great Bible characters as Abraham, Moses, Job, Gideon, John the Baptist, Peter, Martha, including the chief of them all, doubting Thomas, but as Joel Osteen counseled, "you don't sit around meditating on them."

However, the Bible characters mentioned above, overcame their doubts and fears in various ways. Abraham conquered his fear and doubt by believing God's words, Genesis 15:6; Moses by seeing God's glory Exodus 33:32-33; Gideon by throwing out the fleece Judges 6: 38-40 and John the Baptist by seeing Christ miracles Mathew 11:4-6.

In the same vein, Peter ended his doubt by reaching out to Christ as represented in Mathew 14:30-31 and Thomas by seeing and touching the risen Jesus, John 20:26-28.

The above examples show that you can also overcome your doubt and fear, especially by the living word which is *"alive, and active, sharper than any double-edge sword."* Hebrews 4: 12

Mason has a very good advice here, he says when fear knocks at your door, "let faith answer because worry doesn't help tomorrow's troubles, but ruin today's happiness."

Another reason we need faith uplift is that **it is the primary condition of our justification.**

When God justifies, He declares Believers in Christ to be righteous in spite of their sins. To be justified is to be in right standing with God Almighty.

In Romans 3: 21-28, the scriptures record that Abraham believed God and it was credited to him as righteousness.

Verse 22 states expressly that *"This righteousness is given through faith in Jesus Christ to all who believe."*

A core theme of the Bible is righteousness. It is attained when one accepts Christ, then God in His grace gives the individual the righteousness of Christ. We are made right with God when we believe that Jesus shed his blood and was sacrificed for us sinners. That is why the word of God says that we are justified by faith and not by works.

When one is living a life of righteousness, one gets bold in faith and will be able to approach the throne of grace. This is very different from when one is living in sin; one lacks the courage even to pray. Prayers give courage, think of it this way, one who kneels before God can stand before anyone.

Lastly and most importantly, it is a well known truth that **without faith, we cannot please God.** Hebrews 11:6.

From creation, man has not really put his entire faith in God Almighty. The reason for instance, the serpent was able to convince Adam and Eve, the reason the Israelites assembled their jewelries to make a god, the reason they wanted a king even against the will of God, the reason they did not believe in and indeed crucified the mediator, Jesus Christ and the reason even while with Christ, it explains why the disciples were still afraid.

However, the few that have attempted to put their entire faith in God reaped bountifully, which is why Abraham believed God and it was counted for him as righteousness, Noah in spite of the ridicule, built the ark, David triumphed over Goliath, Zachariah had a son at old age, the woman with the issue of blood was healed, Peter walked on water and so on.

It should be noted that from the onset, God made it very clear that *"For I the Lord your God, am a jealous God,"* Exodus 20:5, and that we should have no other gods before Him.

It therefore goes without saying that God must be first in all we do, in all we say and even conceive. That would show the faith we have in Him. Some people, either out of lack of knowledge or stubbornness of heart have gone ahead without the Lord and when they get their fingers burnt, and if fortunate to be alive, live in regrets.

A case in point is in 1 Chronicles 15 when David assembled the Israelites and explained to them why Uzzah died for touching the Ark while being taken to Jerusalem. The chapter told us how David learnt from the mistake of not putting God first, *"...our God broke out in anger against us. We did not inquire of him about how to do it in the prescribed way."* I Chron 15:13

It follows therefore as accentuated by Apostle Paul, anyone that comes to God MUST believe that He is God Almighty, the one who is, who was and who is to come; there is no other god before and after Him, also He rewards those who diligently seek Him.

Faith in God and not facts should propel us to action because our faith connects our downsides, our inadequacies to God's strength, and with God nothing is impossible. We should always have in mind that things with God are the truth and not just facts.

CHAPTER 5

POWER OF THE MIND

The mind is the epicenter of the body. It is the engine room of the human body and is responsible for why people do what they do, act the way they do and respond in one way or the other to situations and make one choice or the other.

During a sermon I gave in our local church in Long Island, New York. I shared with the congregation that the mind or heart as the case may be, is the bastion, upholder, citadel of an individual's good or sinful nature.

I went on to explain that while we take the head to be the center of human activities, the Bible describes the heart of man as the wellspring of the body, where all things spring from, both good and bad. Proverbs 4:23

This is largely because the mind controls our intellect, thought pattern according to Psalm 19:14, our emotions Acts 2:26, and our will 2 Chronicles 6:7.

This goes to explain why Pastor Adeboye states that "the challenge of most Believers is not how to avoid open sins, but how to stay righteous in their thought realm."

Joyce Meyer in a special edition of her ministry magazine, Enjoying Everyday Life said that "the mind is the battlefield where we win or lose in life," that is why some are experts in their chosen fields of endeavor, while others struggle to barely make it.

Take for instance King Saul, he was, most probably terror stricken at the mention of the name Goliath. Goliath had become a thorn in the flesh of the king as he constantly taunted and challenged the Israelites to battle but nobody was bold enough to respond, not even the king.

However, the king became an expert in dressing up little David for the battle when David volunteered to face Goliath and take the shame away from the Israelites. I Samuel 17:38-39.

In the same vein, the mind accounts for why some people with impressive credentials, rich contacts and accumulated skills may end up always getting ready, but never get started.

The mind creates emotions and makes one either love, hate or afraid of someone or circumstances. That is principally why the scriptures in Proverbs 23:7 say that, for as a man thinks in his heart so he is.

It also affects our thought patterns and affects our behaviors, a reason why two persons see the same thing but react very differently.

The story of spies sent out in Numbers 13 offers an apt example of how mindset can make or mar an individual, group or nation.

The response of the spies to what they saw gives vent to one of our earlier definitions of faith as how big or small your God is. Ten of the spies became so scared of the Anaks, developing a grasshopper mentality, while two believed the Anaks could be defeated.

The ten spies had an indomitable perception of the descendants of Anaks, while the remaining two, Caleb and Joshua saw them as conquerable.

One can even sense the urgency in the minority's report, *"We should go up and take possession of the land, for we can certainly do it."* Numbers 13:30. It is often said that what you call it, is what it is.

The scenario answers the questions: Is God big enough to save you when the going gets tough? Or do you expect too much or too little of God, a question posed by Fred Kinsney and Ken Wade in their book, "What to Do When your World Falls Apart."

Considering our thought patterns

In discussing our thought patterns, it is useful to know that the heart is the wellspring of the body; it is the seat of intellect, emotions and defines the individual.

This is because more often than not, it is what is conceived in the heart or mind that comes out of the mouth when an individual speaks. The speech then defines the thought process of the individual which could be positive or negative. A reason why the scripture states that *"What goes into someone's mouth does not defile them, but what comes out of their mouth, that is what defiles them."* Mathew 15: 11

Psychologists say that our emotions, behavior are not necessarily dependent on what is going on around us in our environment but that something else is at work that determines responses to life situations and that thing is ---- our thought pattern, belief system.

Prominent in this line of thought is the work of Albert Ellis. Ellis, considered by many as the father of cognitive therapies, originally formulated the ABC model of emotions to describe the manner in which our environment impacts our emotional and behavioral reactions.

Ellis, 1962 argued that human beings for the most part create their own emotional consequences. From his perspective, when a highly charged emotional consequence (C) follows a significant activating event (A), it might seem that A causes C. Yet, in actuality, emotional consequences are largely created by (*B*), the individual's belief system. (*A*), filtered through (*B*), leads to (*C*).

The model was highly accepted over the years and although it has gone through many modifications, the underlying principle that our belief system or environment influences our thought process defines the individual, has some biblical tones.

It is like this for example: *1. (A) Pastor didn't return my phone calls. (C) Pastor did not return my call because I am not important to him.*

(C) here represents my disappointment, outcome of unreturned calls.

2. Janet didn't invite me to her birthday party (A)

I think it's because we had a disagreement the last time (C)

In the above examples, the B is left out. Incidentally, B is a very important element of the thinking process. According to Ellis, (B) is bedrock of the thought process, mindset, self-talk, belief systems the home of our emotions, which is what gives room to (C).

Let's take another look at one of the examples above with the (B) now included.

Pastor didn't return my phone calls (A)

Possible reasons (B):

    (i)   *He is now avoiding me.*
    (ii) *He doesn't really care about me.*
    (iii) *Because I stopped working in church*
    (iv) *He is now working two jobs*
    (v) *Am not in the church inner circle etc*

All the variables in (B) above give the outcome that "Pastor did not return my call because I am not important to him (C)"

Thus giving the complete model of A+B=C

Ellis model points out that the thought pattern, belief system, self-talk, perspective of the individual, which is (B) gave rise to the conclusion in (C), which could be right or wrong, helpful or destructive.

The point here is that what and how an individual thinks, which constitutes the perspective, is a very powerful influence on the individual, it makes or mars the individual; it makes the individual have faith deficiency, little faith or great faith. A biblical perspective of this is in Proverbs 23:7 which says "*for as he thinks in his heart so is he.*"

The import of the above analysis is that in building our faith, the power of perspective is very important. The individual's perspective of God, knowledge of His ability, power, love, mercy, awesomeness and faithfulness becomes very paramount.

In the midst of what Job was going through, his perspective of God was *"For I know that my Redeemer lives"* Job 19:25 and it helped him overcome his grief.

Our thought pattern affects/create our emotions

Philosophers as accentuated by Epictetus say that men are disturbed not by things, but by the view they take of them.

In each and every situation, one's response is based on how the individual chooses to interpret the event or circumstances, which is determined by perception, perspective and emotions.

Emotions vary, and could range from depression to misery, happiness, fear, love, hatred, hope, hopelessness etc.

It is however pertinent to point out here that some people do not believe emotion has any place in the ways of God. This school of thought sees emotion as something negative, and more of a curse than a blessing.

Others though say that emotion has a place in the salvation race. Prominent among those in this school of thought is Dr Bob Kellemen, founder of RPM Ministries. According to Kellemen, "emotions were God's idea. Not only did He give them to us; He experiences them Himself. God is an emotional being. Read that again. Don't dodge it. *God is an emotional being.* God the Father gets angry. God the Son weeps. God the Spirit grieves. The Trinity emotes."

He substantiates his position from how the Psalmist describes God's utmost care in creating us in Psalm 139:13. He also referenced Psalm 73:21 and Proverbs 23:16 as directly relating to emotions. Emotions, he indicated, are windows to the soul and reveals our continuous search to know God.

Apparently agreeing with Kellemen, Stoop uses Lamentations 3: 1-24 NIV to give a vivid illustration of how our thoughts create our emotions as expressed by Jeremiah the prophet.

[1] I am the man who has seen affliction
   by the rod of the LORD's wrath.

[2] He has driven me away and made me walk
   in darkness rather than light;

[3] indeed, he has turned his hand against me
   again and again, all day long.

[4] He has made my skin and my flesh grow old
   and has broken my bones.

[5] He has besieged me and surrounded me
   with bitterness and hardship.

[6] He has made me dwell in darkness
   like those long dead.

[7] He has walled me in so I cannot escape;
   he has weighed me down with chains.

⁸ Even when I call out or cry for help,
   he shuts out my prayer.

⁹ He has barred my way with blocks of stone;
   he has made my paths crooked.

¹⁰ Like a bear lying in wait,
   like a lion in hiding,

¹¹ he dragged me from the path and mangled me
   and left me without help.

¹² He drew his bow
   and made me the target for his arrows.

¹³ He pierced my heart
   with arrows from his quiver.

¹⁴ I became the laughingstock of all my people;
   they mock me in song all day long.

¹⁵ He has filled me with bitter herbs
   and given me gall to drink.

¹⁶ He has broken my teeth with gravel;
   he has trampled me in the dust.

¹⁷ I have been deprived of peace;
   I have forgotten what prosperity is.

¹⁸ So I say, "My splendor is gone
   and all that I had hoped from the LORD."

¹⁹ I remember my affliction and my wandering,
    the bitterness and the gall.

²⁰ I well remember them,
    and my soul is downcast within me.

²¹ Yet this I call to mind
    and therefore I have hope:

²² Because of the LORD's great love we are not consumed,
    for his compassions never fail.

²³ They are new every morning;
    great is your faithfulness.

²⁴ I say to myself, "The LORD is my portion;
    therefore I will wait for him."

²⁵ The LORD is good to those whose hope is in him,
    to the one who seeks him;

In verses 1-3, Jeremiah the prophet is in misery and hopelessness. He believes God is against him.

In verse 4, he still expresses depression.

In verses 5-6, he feels trapped by the vicissitudes of life.

In verses 7-9, Jeremiah expresses how God is just against him.

In verses 10-15, he points out that he is now a laughing stock, suffering dejection.

In verse 16-17, his happiness, if any, is all gone.

In verse 18, depression sets in.

However in verses 19-20, he begins to change his perspective, thought pattern.

In verse 21, a ray of hope sets in.

From verses 22-24, he has moved from despair, to mountain top of faith.

In verse 24, he remembers the faithfulness of God and hope takes over.

It could be seen from this exposition, that Jeremiah's thought pattern created his emotions and made him regain self control.

Although nothing had changed within his immediate environment, this great illustration shows how his emotions navigated from hopelessness to hopefulness and expectancy even within the same time frame.

Going back to our earlier illustration therefore, it could be seen that the emotional consequences of any activity are not created by any event. C is not caused by A, it is rather caused by the perception, world view and perspective of the individual, which is the B.

This belief system, perception, helps to either increase or decrease one's faith in God's ability to save the individual. It can therefore be stated that it is our mindset, thought pattern that explains why someone can experience inner rest and peace of mind in the midst of the most trying circumstances in life and others do not.

It is also the reason one can ignore all the positive pleasant events occurring in one's life and become worried, miserable to death and vice versa. That is what I meant earlier when I warned that we should not meditate on our worries or fears as pointed out by Mason, because as he puts it, "too much analysis leads to paralysis."

The lesson here is that we cannot be passive or pessimistic about our faith in God and expect to experience a manifestation of his resurrection power in our life.

We must therefore make every effort to activate our faith by feeding on God's promises that are everywhere in the Bible.

John Maxwell sums it up that when we keep our head and heart going in the right direction, we won't have to worry about our feet.

CHAPTER 6

THE FAITH LIFT

From the illustrations given in the previous chapter, one sure way to increase our faith is to **Have positive confession:** The scriptures say explicitly that out of the abundance of the heart that the mouth speaks. The makeup of one's thought process and perspective, constitute our confessions.

Charles Stanley in, <u>Living the Extraordinary Life</u>, points out that David made positive confessions of faith to those around him when he asked those around him, *"who is this uncircumcised Philistine, that he should taunt the armies of the living God?"* 1 Samuel 17:26. To Saul he said, *the Lord who delivered me from the paw of the lion and the paw of the bear will rescue me from the hand of this Philistine* 1 Samuel 17:37 and to Goliath he said, *"I come against you in the name of the Lord almighty, the God of the armies of Israel, whom you have defied."* 1 Samuel 17:45. David was apparently loaded with an avalanche of positive confessions.

An individual is largely a product of his/her own thoughts, because as a man thinks so he is and belief is said to be the thermostat that regulates what we accomplish in life.

Conversely, disbelief is generally agreed to be a negative power; when the mind doubts, it introduces excuses and attracts reasons to support failure.

We can harness the power of believe through the living word of God. How?

This is how it works, one cannot use what one does not have. This was why Joshua counseled that we should meditate daily on the word so as to use it to make our ways prosperous. Joshua 1:8. Those who are familiar with Psalm 23 know that it is a storehouse of positive confessions. In Psalm 23, David penned that those who delight in the word and meditate on them day and night shall have everlasting prosperity.

Our faith is strengthened by repeated meditation upon the word. Early faith teacher, Charles Spurgeon (1834-1892) instructed that Believers should take up the shield of faith by repeating God's promises, declaring the glorious doctrines of faith, proclaiming insights from scriptural illustrations and recounting how God has acted on their behalf before now.

However, while strongly recommending positive confession, another faith scholar, Hannah Smith warns against trying to make an incantation or magical formula out of positive confession.

According to Smith, "we must not say it with our lips only, and then our actions deny our words. We must say it with our whole being, with thought, word and action."

Confession therefore should be an attitude from the heart, body and soul. Psalm 130: 5-6 puts it this way, *" I wait for the Lord, my whole being waits, and in his word I put my hope. I wait for the Lord, more than watchmen wait for the morning."* My emphasis there means one's body soul and spirit.

Putting faith in God should not just be lip service or a magic formula where one puts God in a spirit box and expects Him to act in a predicted way to suit our wishes at our own time.

Although Apostle Peter wrote very little in the Bible, but his messages are very instructive. Peter sums it up *"Humble yourselves, therefore, under God's mighty hand, that he may lift you up in due time. Cast all your anxiety on him because he cares for you."*1Peter5:6-7

Waiting on the Lord has never been a time wasting endeavor.

Action Point: God is definitely not waiting to act on our command, we should learn from Habakkuk's way of clinging or resting on God, irrespective of circumstances. Habakkuk 3:16-19

Another way of increasing our faith is to **Have passion in what we do:** Moses in his valedictory speech told the Israelites in Deuteronomy 10:12 to serve the Lord *"with all your heart and with all your soul."*

Deep interest and passion in anything produce faith in that activity. But where there is a passing interest, discouragement easily sets in from the slightest upset. Do not water down your passion based on circumstances around you because the circumstances can change.

Solomon in Ecclesiastics 9:10 advises that *"whatever your hand finds to do, do it with all your might."* Jesus showed considerable passion in carrying out his assignment on earth.

Everyone has something he or she loves, and we are motivated by what we love. When we add passion to emotion, to belief, it becomes a conviction, and gives us a breakthrough.

Most sportsmen for instance love their games and all they do is add passion to it and they become celebrities.

Mike Murdock says that what generates passion and zeal in you is a clue to revealing your destiny, adding that nothing significant is achieved without passion.

According to John Mason, "most winners are just ex-losers who got passionate." You must know that power follows passion.

Every innovator must have a stimulant; what is yours? Passion produces faith and faith produces power. That is exactly what was responsible for the success of Apostle Paul in his ministry. He had great passion for the work, which increased his faith in spite of adversaries. 1 Corinth 16:9.

Action Point: Stop and think about what grabs your attention and prayerfully pursue it with faith and passion.

Go the extra mile: One way of increasing one's faith is in going the extra mile and not settling for the average through complacency.

In Genesis 24, all Abraham's servant asked for was a little water to drink in verse 17. *…please let me drink a little water from your jar."*

Rebecca not only gave him water to drink, but also gave the ten camels water to drink. Each camel drinks at least 10 jars, which means she fetched at least 100 jars on a simple request and God honored her effort.

By that singular action, Rebecca worked herself into the lineage of Christ and the covenant. Through your persistence, passion and faith, you too can work your way into the kingdom of light where prosperity and everlasting joy abound.

The story in Mark 2:1-5 where the paralytic man was lowered through the roof for healing by Jesus is a great example of going the extra mile. Ordinarily, they would have given up, but they went the extra mile by going through the roof and their faith in Jesus Christ was rewarded. As you read this book and take that step of faith, God will reward your faith in Jesus mighty name.

What is your attitude to service, to giving, to holiness? Do not ignore the unction of the Holy Spirit urging you to do a little more, give a little more and hang in there for God's due time. 1 Peter 5:6.

Action Point: Do not relax or give up so soon, see every task as the last opportunity to make a mark, you may be nearer than you think. Remember faith is not found in comfort zones.

Rejoice in your sufferings: James 1:2 gives a very good grounding in profiting from trials. The passage encourages us to, *"Consider it pure joy, my brothers and sisters,[whenever you face trials of many kinds "* because as Apostle Paul puts it, great doors are opened with many adversaries, opposition 1 Corinthians 16:9.

Life opportunities do more often than not, come wrapped in adversities, challenges. Great faith scholar of old, Hudson Taylor (1832-1905) said that, "difficulties are the proving ground of faith; they give faith nourishment and strength."

Taylor sees faith as something that grows by exercising it, adding that "faith is impossible without a trial." Remember also the old adage that it gets darkest shortly before dawn.

Jentezen Franklin believes that, "your problem is the key to your promotion. The reason the pressure has been turned up is because you are so close to your victory. You are too close to give up."

Joel Osteen points out that if you are not uncomfortable once in a while, then you are not really using your faith. Faith, according to him, is all about stretching.

Your obstacles, challenges and opportunities may seem intimidating, but God would not have presented them to you if he had not known already that you have what it takes to overcome. *"No temptation has overtaken you except what is common to mankind. And God is faithful; he will not let you be tempted beyond what you can bear. But when you are tempted, he will also provide a way out so that you can endure it."* 1 Corinthians 10:13

Action Point: Step out of your comfort zone and take steps of faith to bring out the treasure buried in you. God expects us to do what we can and He will do what we can't.

Unsettling traumatic experience: Although no one prays for a traumatic experience to increase one's faith, but not many things help muster faith as an incident that one escaped by a skin breath.

When the situation is such that you know that if not for God, you would have been consumed, then your faith in God rises astronomically and He becomes your rock of ages, your Alpha and Omega, your beginning and your end.

It could as well be a positive experience, say a miracle. For instance there is nothing anyone could have told the blind man in John 9 to change his gratefulness to Jesus Christ. He told those questioning him, *"Whether he is a sinner or not, I don't know. One thing I do know is that I was blind but now I see."* John 9:25. To such an individual, it is Jesus Christ or nothing and no one else.

Not even further castigation could persuade him from affirming the authority of Christ as he bluntly added in John 9:33 that, "…*if this man were not from God, he could do nothing.*"

Action Point: Pray that God gives you a miracle that will increase your faith and unsettle your adversaries.

Sowing seed of faith. The sowing of seed of faith should be a regular activity among practicing Christians; same thing with making a vow to God Almighty. When there are answers to the petition that warranted the seed or vow, one's perspective of God changes and faith increases.

A vow is a solemn promise made to God in anticipation of something to happen. While Jacob was running away after stealing Esau's blessings in Genesis 28, he made a vow that if he can return safely to his father; he will give a tenth of everything God gives him.

Instances abound in the Bible where people used vows to get what they wanted. A case in point is in the case of Hannah.

Hannah made a vow by sowing a seed to have a son. "And she made a vow, saying, "*Lord Almighty, if you will only look on your servant's misery and remember me, and not forget your servant but give her a son, then I will give him to the Lord for all the days of his life, and no razor will ever be used on his head.*" 1 Samuel 1:11. Such statements can only come from one with an utmost faith.

The seed varies according to the individual. It could be money, an asset, time, skills etc.

How it works is that vows are mostly made in time of distress or when someone is in dire need as reflected in Psalm 66: 13- 14; and it is often very voluntary Deuteronomy 23: 21-23. King Solomon pointed out however in Ecclesiastes 5:5 that it is better to say nothing than to promise something that you won't follow through.

Sowing of seeds and making vows are biblical principles. Such seeds must cost the sower something, and most times sown in tears. Psalm 126:5.

The warning here though is that one must be sensitive to the Holy Spirit so as to sow in a good soil.

God is ever faithful. 1 Corinthians 1: 9. When we sow or make a vow, during the intervening time of waiting, our faith should be high; on the upbeat knowing that He is the only one that can see us through whatever we are passing through.

Action Point: *Remember that the law of the harvest is to reap more than you sow, try God today by sowing a seed of faith.*

Fervent prayers: Like every other thing in life, one can increase his/her faith by praying. Mark: 11:24 gives a direct link between prayer and faith. The word of God says that the fervent prayers of a righteous man avail much.

Again, one of our definitions of faith as how big or small your God is, comes to bear here. God answers prayers, which is why David in Psalm 55:17 acknowledges that at whatever time he calls on God, the Lord hears him, rescues him and indeed faithfully answers our prayers with awesome deeds, Psalm 65: 5.

The act of praying shows our hope and trust in God and a faith-based prayer is that with our eyes focused on God and not on the problem.

Striking a relationship between prayer and faith has been extensively discussed by some Bible scholars. According to Paul King, faith is not only expressed through prayer, but prayer actually energizes and activates faith, taking it to new heights.

Edward Bounds, known as God's Prayer Warrior said that true prayer is an operation of faith, as there is no real prayer without faith and no real faith without prayers.

Bounds adds that, " faith is only omnipotent when it is on its knees."

In the same vein, Jentezen Franklin believes that prayers take us where we can't go in person, it outlives those who utter them; therefore prayers are deathless and outlive a generation, an age and a people.

F.B Meyer once said that "the great tragedy of life is not unanswered prayer, but unoffered prayer.

Martin Luther points out that frequent kneeling will keep you in good standing with God and as I pointed out earlier, one who kneels before God in prayers can stand before anyone, anytime any where.

Action Point: Do deep praying before you find yourself in a deep hole. Sometimes we think we are too busy to pray, that is a great mistake, for praying is actually a saving of time.

Above all, **to increase our faith, we must exercise it**. The scripture in 2 Corinthians 5: 7 says we must *"live by faith and not by sight."* This is very important as faith gives us the courage to face the present with confidence and the future with expectancy. This is for those who do not want to spend their today living with a chicken mentality of being afraid of everything, but soar high with brevity to fulfill their destiny.

John mason points out that true faith has hands and feet, it takes action and it is not enough to know that you know, it is important to show that you know.

Pastor Adeboye in one of his several teachings advises that, "to get God's best, you must be prepared to disengage your senses and engage faith."

Adeboye counsels that you can hear the inaudible if you apply your spiritual hears, and be ready to hear His word and do it, be prepared to wait on him.

Action Point: when you apply your faith, you will feel God, you can touch Him with your hands and you will not remain the same.

CHAPTER 7

WHEN GOD DOES NOT SPEAK

Ordinarily, this little book would have well ended with the last chapter, but it is imperative to counsel against disillusionment when things do not happen as at when and how we want it. Remember that it is God's own time and not yours.

Abraham waited for 25 years between the promise and the birth of Isaac, David was anointed as a teenager, but it took years for him to actually ascend the throne. Peter told us in one of his short writings about God's due time 1 Peter 5:6, and since God knows the end from the beginning, it does make great sense to wait on Him.

Putting one's entire trust in God presupposes that God will answer one's prayers. However, some people have experienced the frustrations of seemingly unanswered prayers. The frustrations could be very apparent and inflicting, more especially when the individual is overwhelmed with grief and continuously pours his/her heart to God Almighty but nothing seems to be happening.

This must have been the state of the writer of Psalm 102 who was so afflicted that he said in the eleventh verse that, *"my days are like the evening shadow; I wither away like grass."*

Are you getting frustrated having anxiously waited to hear from God on a particular issue, but encountering God's silence?

Moses was very direct in Deuteronomy 8: 2 when he urged the Israelites to *"Remember how the LORD your God led you all the way in the wilderness these forty years, to humble and test you in order to know what was in your heart, whether or not you would keep his commands."*

God's silence to some could be for a short time, to others for a long time. The Israelites cried for 400 years unto God, the man at the pool of Bethesda waited for 38 years while the Canaanite woman waited for just a little while.

It sure behooves on God to answer when He wants to.

However, one thing is certain, God is always speaking; we are the ones not listening. Even when we think God is not speaking, He is listening. Exodus 3:7 for instance states that, *"The LORD said, "I have indeed seen the misery of my people in Egypt. I have heard them crying out because of their slave drivers, and I am concerned about their suffering."*

Would a loving God be silent?

This is a question that many committed Christians may have trouble dealing with especially when asked by a new convert.

Put in another way, why would a loving God allow His people to suffer and undergo pains, persecution, challenges and adversity? The questions become very relevant because the scripture says that *"each heart knows its own bitterness."* Proverbs 14: 10.

Some Bible portions such as Psalms 5:1-3, 13, 22: 1-2, 55:1-2, Psalm 88, 102 and many more all sound like distress calls of one afflicted.

It is therefore not strange that you may have been entertaining this thought because Gideon even confronted God directly with same question in Judges 6: 13, *"Pardon me my Lord, but if the Lord is with us, why has all this happened to us?*

A plausible reason that John Stott volunteers is that "suffering undoubtedly constitutes the greatest challenge to the Christian faith."

From one of the smallest, but also one of the most impactful books I have ever read, Mart De Haan gives a very sound perspective on why a loving God may be silent when you are undergoing what I called your wilderness experience.

In the book, " Why Would a Good God Allow Suffering," Haan points out that as much as we may abhor pain, we have to admit that it often serves a good purpose as God uses the pain to alert us to serious problems. Pains, Haan indicated, sounds the alarm, indicating that something is wrong somewhere, it could be with the world, humanity or the individual. Hebrews 12: 5-6.

When all is not well, adversity helps direct us to seek for the solution in God, 2 Corinthians 1:8-9, to appropriate God's grace which is available for us 2 Corinthians 12:9.

Apostle Paul in his letter to the Romans pointed out that pains and trials also serve to shape us to be more mature in faith Romans 5:3-5 as well as show us how much we need each other to survive. 1Corinthians 12.

From the above perspective therefore, it could be said that lack of communication between God and man could mean that God is either not speaking when you want Him to or man is not listening.

We must be reminded that God does not owe any man, and He is not a man that He should lie. He, therefore answers our prayers (for those who pray anyway) in His own manner and time.

As earlier pointed out, God is not a magical spirit and cannot be put into any genie box to act how we want. God is not waiting to act on our command, but rather we must rest on Him and emulate Bible characters as Habakkuk and Job who clung to Him irrespective of the circumstances. *"Though the fig tree does not bud and there are no grapes on the vines, though the olive crop fails and the fields produce no food, though there are no sheep in the pen and no cattle in the stalls, yet I will rejoice in the LORD, I will be joyful in God my Savior. The Sovereign LORD is my strength; he makes my feet like the feet of a deer, he enables me to tread on the heights."* Habakkuk 3:17-19.

Job also made similar reference in Job 38: 1-12, 42:1-6.

In one of the most compelling books on faith that I have read, "The Blessings of Adversity," Barry Black alluded why God is often silent to some of these reasons. Sin: Isaiah 59: 1-3, stubbornness 1 Sam 8: 18 or we may even be unprepared to hear from God as it happened to boy Samuel 1 Sam 3: 1-7.

To others, it may be that they feel they have waited too long already and start seeking for alternatives, just as King Saul did in 1 Samuel 13:8-15 thereby wavering in faith: Romans 4: 20-22.

Also, because God looks at the heart, He sees our selfish motives James 4:3, 2 Chronicles 12 and cannot answer such prayers.

Note this: God is not likely to speak when one is undergoing a test 1 Peter 1:7, James 1:3. Remember, the teacher is always silent during an exam session. What you get during exams is always the instructions and in this case the Bible exists to give us all the needed instructions.

God may also be silent in your case because it is not His appointed time: Acts 1:7, this is why Peter counselled,

"Humble yourselves, therefore, under God's mighty hand, that he may lift you up in due time." 1 Peter5: 6.

Those before You

Like Apostle Paul said, you are not experiencing anything strange if God has been silent in your circumstances. This is because many Bible characters experienced God's silence at one time or the other:

Abraham in Genesis 22 travelled for three days heeding the instruction of God to go sacrifice his son, his only son, Isaac; but God eventually spoke.

In the process of time, a new King emerged in Egypt who put the Israelites in bondage and they cried unto God for so many years and God heard their groaning and remembered them. Exodus 2: 23-24.

For two years, the person Joseph hoped on, forgot to mention him to the King, but with time it happened according to Genesis 41.

The woman with the issue of blood was with that infirmity for twelve years Mark 5: 25, but one day she was made whole.

Mary and Martha had to deal with the Lord's silence when their brother Lazarus died before Jesus showed up four days later. John 11: 22-25

Dealing with God's Silence

We must therefore learn to deal with God's silence and reap the blessings of trusting God even when it seems He's silent. He will surely break His silence, Psalm 33:9, Palms 148:5-6.

In dealing with the period God is not speaking, Black points out that we need to muster **Patience**, which is the staying power of an individual to hang in there waiting on God. *The Psalmist said "I waited patiently for the Lord; he turned to me and heard my cry."* Psalm 40:1

God cannot be said to be slow because He controls the times and seasons; more so when the race is not for the swift. Life experiences show that those who want to go ahead of God's time table always get their fingers burnt and at times it may be too late to retreat from the haste.

God's patience to mankind is unequalled because He is slow to anger, abandoning in love, forgiving our numerous sins and rebellious ways Numbers 14:18.

Apostle Paul counseled that we should be patient especially during affliction and faithful in prayer. God usually steps in at the end, just before you descend to your deepest depths, the Lord will step in. Remember that He was there when the furnace was being heated for Daniel, He was there before Lazarus died, but He stepped in at last and there was deliverance.

Nowhere in the Bible is the spiritual trait of **Perseverance** better illustrated than in the story of faith of the Canaanite Woman in Mathew 15: 21-25.

In modern day lifestyle with all our self worth we carry about, the woman would have felt ignored when Jesus did not answer her at the first instance.

Secondly, she would have felt highly insulted when the disciples urged Jesus to send her away for constituting a nuisance.

To worsen her situation, Jesus bluntly told the woman that He was not sent to her but to the lost adding that it is not right to take the children's food to the dogs, an inference anybody would feel offended.

But there lies the persistence as the woman replied that " *even the dogs eat the crumbs that fall from their masters table.*" Mathew 15:27

At this response Jesus was overwhelmed with the woman's level of faith and exclaimed, *"Woman, you have great faith! Your request is granted."* Mathew 15:28. This is perseverance; the woman did not give up. She persisted and got what she needed.

If you persist, God will do the same for you. Perseverance is an outstanding characteristic in building one's faith and it is akin to our earlier definition of faith as putting all our eggs in God's basket.

Subscribe to the word

The scriptures say that in the beginning was the word and the word was with God. Moses in his valedictory speech in

Deuteronomy 32: 47 said God's words are not idle or mere words, *"they are your life,"* and John tells us how the word became flesh. Apostle Paul adds in 1 Corinthians 1:18 that the word is the power of God. All these add up to encourage us to hold on to God's words which are His promises to mankind.

Has God ever spoken to you through His word? Then hold on to it, for it will come to pass. On the other hand, you don't seem to understand what is happening, although you are sure you heard clearly from God, but you are still in your wilderness, such as David, Joseph, Moses found themselves before their destinies were actualized.

Bear in mind that during your time of test, the best option is to get back to the examination instructions, which are in the Bible for guide to an appropriate response.

To others, it may be that they do not hear God speak, then in that case read about Him. When you can't hear God, read God, because according to Black, "When God is silent in your life, find answers in His word."

Zechariah 9:12, Isaiah 41: 10, Philippians 4:13 are very few examples of God speaking to someone. If you claim it, it sure works for you.

Activate your faith: the synonyms for activate includes turn on, trigger, stimulate, set in motion etc, that means in responding to God's silence, one must work on one's faith that has been dormant.

Since God in His words does not promise an explanation but that He will be with us and see us through, all we need do is to put our faith to work. Interestingly, we all have an atom of faith in us. It is left to us to stimulate or trigger it into motion.

That is why Jesus told the blind man, "*according to your faith, let it be done to you and their sight was restored,*" Mathew 9:29

It is good to know that when you put faith into action, God will go to work on your behalf and that God will not reveal the second step until you have taken the first step.

Paul in telling the Romans about the faith of Abraham said that in spite of all the challenges, delays even after the promise, Abraham was "*fully persuaded that God had power to do what He had promised.*" Romans 4:21.

This is why as Believers, we should all subscribe to David's instruction in Psalm 27: 13 that we should wait for the Lord, be strong and courageous and wait for Him for He will do what He says He will do in your life.

Remember that without the cross, there would be no crown. Work for the crown with steadfast steps holding on to the Believers rod—faith.

Psalm 23: 1-3, Psalm 84: 11, James 1: 2-4, Philippians: 1:6, Job 38, Numbers 11: 23, Isaiah 55:10-11